Living by Troubled Waters

Living by Troubled Waters

Roy McFarlane

Nine
Arches
Press

Living by Troubled Waters
Roy McFarlane

ISBN: 978-1-913437-54-1
eISBN: 978-1-913437-55-8

First published October 2022 by:

Nine Arches Press
Unit 14, Sir Frank Whittle Business Centre,
Great Central Way, Rugby.
CV21 3XH
United Kingdom

www.ninearchespress.com

Nine Arches Press is supported using public funding by Arts Council England.

Supported using public funding by
ARTS COUNCIL
ENGLAND

Contents

Icarus's mouth

the dismembered past

the Clearing

{ }

How we could have lived or died this way, how the descendants of slaves
Still fled and the descendants of slave-catchers still shot them, how we awoke
Every morning without the blood of the dead sweating from every pore.

– Martín Espada, 'How We Could Have Lived or Died This Way'

When we revolt it's not for a particular culture. We revolt simply because,
for many reasons, we can no longer breathe.

– Frantz Fanon

A Short History of theViolence Visited upon the Black Bodies of the Enslaved

Erasure & Inclusion (to make known) poems – a term that I've devised when looking for the opposite of erasure – have been created in response to researching reports and articles from the 1800 to 1850s from British and Caribbean newspapers. I chose this particular time period because of The Haitian Revolution and The Abolition of the Slave Trade Act 1807, catalysts to the idea of freedom and identity across the African Diaspora which inspired enslaved runaways *to be free.*

The following selection of Erasure & Inclusion (to make known) poems are interwoven and speak to the general body of poems in this collection and are the threads that hold the collection together. As the poems of the present bear witness to the social issues and tragedies visited upon Black bodies of the present, these incidents are rooted in a past that still hasn't been dealt with, and in current times when their being brought to the surface draws indignation and backlash from white society. These poems cannot be read without the stories of the past being found side-by-side.

First, let me take you back to my childhood; during times of boredom, difficult questions and affirmation of my faith, my mother would say *Go and read your Bible*, a big old cream Bible that held the sixty-six books of the canon but also the apocrypha – the hidden stories between the Old and New Testament. Also, in this hefty tome there were illustration panels interwoven, Rembrandt's works of art inspired by biblical stories, the humanity and passion of the stories (made known) in paintings and drawings. These were images I'd come back to time and time again, lost in the toe-curling *Blinding of Samson* or the body of Christ lovingly and carefully taken down in *Descent from the Cross.*

That framework has followed me into this collection. These Erasure & Inclusion poems bring life to the collection. And as Tom Phillip, one of the early exponents of erasure poems, said in his classical *A Humument*, "I mined and undermined its text to make it yield alternative stories". I wanted the alternative stories of the enslaved runaways, I wanted to draw out their experience and when I couldn't find an erasure poem, I went for the opposite to include an alternative story within the text by shredding, cutting and repeating the text to make known something anew. Erasure & Inclusion (to make known) poems are ways of speaking to, radically intervening in, and responding to the original text in order to draw something out, and find a new voice in the process.

Roy McFarlane,
June 2022.

An aubade in response to *how do you feel* in the wake of George Floyd's death, realising I'm holding a scream, decibels high enough to crack the fragility of white people

I would not write
if it wasn't for a new morning
where canals cut deep enough
to make new waters; where
coots with chicks fill a nest
in a curtain of grass; where
dandelions' breath fills the air;
where herons walk like deities
heads held high and Gregory Porter
takes me to another place:
take me to the alley,
take me to the afflicted ones.

This new morning
barely casts a shadow,
sun gentle, cajoling me
where the River Tame stays true
to the old ways; where the question
rings *will things ever change;*
where an old Black sage who has seen
the knee, the choke, the rope
around the neck – heard the refrain
I can't breathe again and again
tells you *I'm tired.*
I wish for a sun
to rise with the same warmth
as the sun that rises on you, a sun
that shakes hands with the night
and bids us well until the next day.

{   }

The *Black Mother* within each of us – the poet – whispers in our dreams: I feel, therefore I can be free

– Audre Lorde

You are Impossible to Love (Part 1)

Windrush Generation # Paulette Wilson (died) # Kenneth Williams # Junior Green # Judy Griffith # Windrush Generation # Jeffery Miller # Winston Jones # Dexter Bristol (died) # Windrush Generation # Valerie Baker # Richard Stewart

You are the *child of Windrush,* sweet and bitters. You are the unwanted truth written in the pleats of your mother's summer dress. You are love and lust in the time of the Big Freeze. You are the seasons changing. You are the tears cried through the inquisition of *tell me the name of his father.* You are the growing burden, the choice to be made. You are the unwanted, the invisible.

You are the visible, the wanted. You are another mother's love, the love of her mother and the love of many mothers. You are herstory, the visitations of the spirits, discernment and the psalms of pilgrims with *grips* filled with filigrees of God, and a one-way ticket.

# # #

You are *Windrush,* the wanted in times of trouble, the visible that becomes invisible, to be discarded by a nation. You are the unwanted. You are the hunted down in the middle of the night. You are the imprisoned. You are the boarded flight to a place you have never known.

You are the British citizen whose birthright has been taken twice over. You are the papers and documents lost overnight. You are the one who helped to build this house after the walls came tumbling down. You are the one living by troubled waters. You are the one with no songs of Zion under a weeping willow tree.

Glenda Caesar # Anthony Bryan # Windrush Generation # Renford McIntyre # Leighton Joseph Robinson # Michael Braithwaite # Windrush Generation # Hubert Howard # Sarah O'Connor # Elwaldo Romeo # Whitfield Francis # Windrush Generation

We are a Love Supreme

A bang of a gong, a dance with a saxophone,
cymbals sounding like raindrops
on golden leaves and then the double bass,
double iamb echo of *A Love Supreme*.
One take, one gathering; it was meant to be.
Coltrane's gift, his 'struggle for purity.'

My birth mother searched for a love supreme from the time her mother gave her up to move from rural settings to city; from the time she moved into her father's care where she learned the language of an outsider doesn't translate; from the time she knew she was a discord in the harmony of a happy home; from the time she was a darker shade of mistake to her half-sisters; from the time her father decided to leave her behind to make a life in England.

From rural South to Philly in a house full
of women. Coltrane got lost in Bird magic,
(the shaman of jazz who passed on his sorcery
long before *Kind of Blue*) but to take a hit
from the shaman you'll have to take on
his demons, his devils, and it played
in his veins, rained its finger, tapped
on that stream before finding that right note
and hitting it, he hit it sweet, arched his body
back and played as if the devil was in him.

They told my mother the devil was in her, the devil's in the details; the whispers, the sly comments, the need to be loved, laying down in the heat of passion, rising with guilt inside her, my sister filling her young womb. A womb that gave her family an excuse to send her on a one-way ticket to a place they called the Black Country – her father being the nearest thing to a love supreme – where there was once smoke by day and fire by night; a Tartarian place. This is where they sent my mother.

The upper room where he went cold turkey
for five days Coltrane twisted with the
thought that God would take his gift away.
There he made a promise to be a preacher
of the horn, transcending words, speaking
to souls, playing so many sounds. Years later
in his new home and a new life in Dix Hills,
Coltrane descends from his upper room
after five days with an aura and *A Love Supreme*.

My mother's body was a sheet of sound on a cold winter night where a travelling salesman by day and a preacher in the evenings played a tune *round midnight*, his hands made chords vibrate, made his own sounds in the midst of her sounds, his sax sung loud, fingers along her spine, fingers on her lips, they played through the night. A year later a child finds himself in the company of women: two mothers and a sister. A love supreme.

Mother From Her Child

SELLING A MOTHER FROM HER CHILD.

"Do you often buy the wife without the husband?" "Yes, very often; and frequently, too, they sell me the mother while they keep her children. I have often known them take away the infant from its mother's breast and keep it, while they sold her."—Prof. Andrews, late of the University of N. C., in his recent work on Slavery and the Slave-Trade, p. 147, relates the foregoing conversation with a slave-trader on the Potomac.

Living by Troubled Waters #1

River Mumma is said to live at the fountainhead of large rivers,
where she sits on a rock combing her hair with a golden comb.
   – Jamaican Folklore

My mother – the mother who would later adopt me – lived a gulley and dirt-track away from the river she was born beside. The river she walked to early in the morning as a child to draw water. The river where she sat on stones and played whilst River Mumma watched over her. Here, my mother learned of red rivers that flowed within and out of her in times of seasons. In quiet times she bathed and combed the black Indian roots of her hair. Behind dark bushes, dark eyes poured their desire all over her, unwanted desire that burst within her and over river banks, River Mumma cried. In times of swelling, rivers burst from her womb with a man child, a man child she gave to her mother. My mother returned to the river, to be baptised for the sins before and after. The same river watered the land she was tied to, worked hard during the day and prayed all night for a blessing. River Mumma brought her a gift – a good man who walked out of the river, to share bread and God's words on Sundays. The river that released her and allowed her to cross over when she got married, the river she cried into when her man left to go to England, the river she left to travel a thousand miles to be with her man. My mother nearly drowned in the *Rivers of Blood* speech, she knew rivers of hate that flowed along streets, out of backyards and factories. Prayed for the parting of waters to walk on dry land or the strength to walk on water but she left that to Moses and Jesus. Made a home by those troubled waters, found a child in those waters and made a home strong in love.

River Mumma still
watches over her. Waters
still run deep wherever she goes.

Visitation of the Spirits

NEWCROSS HOSPITAL, 2013: A SCAN REPORT ON THE LUNGS

During those moments when the house stretched
and sighed, Mum would say *I see you and God sees you,*
Old Beelzebub and rebuked him in unknown tongues
she always talked at the devil in the neat folds of the house;
on the wings of disasters and proclaiming *God is good.*
I saw no reason to question her daily conversations
with conspirators, spirits and bugs in the corner of rooms.
I was always safe in her world and loved in this world.
It's only now, after the visitation of friends, sleepless nights,
her third bout of cancer, I intervene and apologise
as she tells the doctors, *I know what you doing,*
and *the Lord sees and knows all that is done in the dark.*

KINGSTON, 1907: IN TIMES OF EARTHQUAKES

Mumma Ranei, with the beautiful Indian hair,
flat chested with nipples so pert and beautiful;
she who drew an overseer off his horse every time
he came a visiting in the heat of the day. *You know*
son, when she was young, she worked in Kingston –
and you'd wait for her to continue, wait for memories
to seep out between meals, sometimes after the reading
of an air mail from Jamaica or worming under the covers
of vermillion-coloured albums to find their way to the surface.
When she touched those black and white photos;
those of her mother and sister, two tall women,
staunched as their clothing, giving rise to more stories.
She was hanging clothes out on a roof top, one day
and the Lawd picked her up and placed her on the ground,
moments before there were a roaring and raging of the earth.
And many reported of the quietness, the sharp
intake of breath of the universe and then the cries
and wailing. Dust flared up whilst buildings collapsed
and *You see how God is merciful, God is good all the time.*

PORT ROYAL, 1692: RICHEST AND WICKEDEST CITY IN THE WORLD

You know son, Port Royal was one of the wickedest cities
in the whole world, warning that the Lord sees all things.
Amongst stories of pirates and buccaneers, there was the tale
of how one man wanted to end slavery, *only one man voted*
against dat wickedness, but dem continue wid dem wicked ways,
but dem never know what God had in store for dem,
And who knows where stories fold into myths and unfold
into truths; *Massa Jesus tek dat man by the scruff of his neck*
and move him out of harm's way. Only for God to return,
tearing the building down and killing everyone. Headlines
report of buildings sunk, boats inland; the living and the dead
floated side by side. Centuries later, a pocket watch reads 11.43,
frozen in time, drawn from the watery ruins of Port Royal.

NEW YEARS EVE, 1920: BEDWARD TO ASCEND TO THE SKIES

Dip dem, Bedward, dip dem / dip dem
in the healing stream. She would sing
of the preacher who said he could fly
– an agitator, a madman, locked in an asylum
for serving the word, seasoned in the spirit
of rebellion and in the blood of the enslaved.
But could they hold him, no son as they gathered
in their thousands outside his house, others
knee deep in Hope River, waiting for *de man*
sitting in a tree top, dressed in white, getting ready to fly.
The people said "The man with no wing seh he going to fly,
seh he going to fly." And mum sings *Dip dem deep,*
but not too deep/ dip dem fi cure bad feeling.

ST THOMAS, 1951: HURRICANE CHARLIE PASSOVER

You should have been there and seen
how the sky was blue before it turned
celestial red, *of how people moved*
to a bigger house, of how they prayed,
of how a hurricane thirsty without water
whipped up a wind through the valleys.
Of how they woke to see the banana
and orange trees laying prostrate
to an island god who passed over the land,
of how rivers swelled, of how people lamented
and breadfruit roasting incensed the air.

THE SMOG OF 1962: LOVE IN THE TIMES OF FOG

Stuck on Dudley Hill, on a bus coming from work
escorted by a conductor with a lamp in a swamp of air –
only in England a few months, my mother was stranded.
The bus no longer moving, everybody coming off:
I intended to stop till morning. She who had known hurricanes
wasn't coming off but my father combing through the smog
checking every bus along the route, until he finally found her,
P, me find you, come, mek we guh home, and together
in the deepest of nights they made their way home.

PARKFIELD ROAD, WOLVERHAMPTON, 2014: THE LAST VISITATION

In your living room, where the bed sits in an unfamiliar place,
morphine pump whirling, you're asking with bulging eyes
Where's Roy? You settle when I draw near you and smile.
Moments later they come for you, one last visitation of the spirits,
with cousin in the kitchen and me drowsing off on the sofa,
I felt a touch on my shoulder
as you lay in peaceful slumber, no more choking
or gasping, hands flailing like a drowning child; instead, you floated
on water, heard me whisper, *it's okay Mum, I know you've got to go,*
I love you. And my cousin throws herself to the ground wailing.

The Passion of the Enslaved / On the Body of a Negro

Of excess
of passion in herself
of life lived
but not of your own
to suffer, to bear,
to endure
of every sunrise
you could not own.

Of every sweat;
of every blood shed.
Lay down in the
coopers' shop.
Lay down
in the valley
of eternal
sunrise.

On the body
of a negro man
William
a runaway.
Died by the
Visitation of God
at the Asylum.

On a negro woman
name unknown.
Died by the
Visitation of God
at the Asylum.

On the body
of a negro woman
Sally.
Died by the
Visitation of God.

God goes a-visiting,
walks into an asylum;
bodies of melano,
walking with those
who talk to the
many voices;
walking with those
that leave broken
bodies; walking
with those who
drift in the husk of
yesterday's breath.

God goes a-visiting
in the place of refuge;
the place of *sylon,*
where no one has
the rights of seizure;
in the place
of sanctuary.

Death goes a-visting
on the bodies
of the melano…
when I die /
Hallelujah by and by /
I'll fly away.

Nanny of the Black Country
wearing Converse All Stars

Woh-oi is the open mouth call,
head raised slightly back,
conch shell deliverance,
set the captives free,
ship-a-oi ending.

Mother Beckford was like a nanny
who slipped sweets in my hands
when nobody was looking, lived
on the ninth floor of Blakenhall flats,
and squeezed in the Austin Allegro
on the way back from church shouting
woh-oi at black cats and near misses.

Woh-oi [grunt]
Woh-oi [grunt]

She was the mad woman of the church
who made her presence known with *woh-oi*
and grunts she would hold deep
in her throat like whole mangoes,
and in the seasons of spirits
when the wind blew,
you'd hear those mangoes
drop, one by one, thump as they hit the floor.

She once thumped a man, broke his nose
for calling her *nigger*, would argue
with the elders when they
looked down on her;
people always looked down on her.

Woh-oi [grunt]
Woh-oi [grunt]

She was *Poco, Obeah,* and *Xaymaca,*
She was Maroon cutting swathes through the air
with her tambourine, holding court
with her drum and her hips
and her bottom catching the spirits.

She was the *mix-up* woman of this world,
                    straddled other worlds
wearing Converse All Stars
in her Sunday dress, pill-box hat
and a gold tooth that punctuated
her smile.

Mothers of Love

I can affirm, that the affections between the mothers and even spurious offspring are very powerful as well as permanent...
  – Edward Kamau Brathwaite, *Folk Culture of the Slaves in Jamaica*

Mothers, wherever they saw us,
always greeted us in love.

Mother Hill folded it
with portions of healings

in the name of Jesus.
Mother Rowe cooked it

in Dutch pots of laughter.
Mother Russell golden brown,

shimmered in the beauty of it.
Mother Dawkins' table

overflowed with it
and toto and rum cake too.

Mother Henry planted it
in pots and tended to them.

Mother Taylor sung and danced
under a moon touched by it.

Mother Caine spoke
in the softness of aloe vera.

Mother Stanley spared
not the rod. Mother Douglas

sent bags of it. Mother Ruby
soaked dried fruits in it

for Christmas cakes. Mother Brown
prayed for rain and rivers of it.

Mother Miller sent it
by air mail from Jamaica.

Mother Foulkes mixed it
with stories and proverbs.

Mother Edwards picked it up
at the market and passed it on

to Mother Campbell who shared
without hesitation and Mother Hill

can be found late at night
folding more for a new day.

Black women don't feel pain

A British doctor, Benjamin Moseley, claimed that black people could bear
surgical operations… to drive home his point, he added, 'I have amputated
the legs of many Negroes who have held the upper part of the limbs themselves.'
  – Claudia Rankine, notes from *Just Us*.

my mother knew that lie as she lay in a hospital bed / throat
butchered / they took away her singing voice which conjured
trebles and quavers / the beats on the page translated into the
sounds in the air / they took away her feminity / they took away
her dignity / leaving her with a scar like a fig sliced open she
would cover in the summertime / the stigmata of her loss

Derricotte speaks of her mother / the labour / the pain / *things got
blurry during the middle passage* / back then Black women weren't
given drugs because *black women were like horses* / *they didn't feel
pain* // my mother told me of Black mothers left alone on hospital
wards / left to endure pain / always enduring pain

*Blisters to my hands, legs and feet, which bear the scars to this day. He
continued until he drew up the dark skin* / John Brown, a slave lent
to Dr Thomas Hilton / to imagine and to formulate all manner of
assumption upon Black bodies / I want to dig under the copious
thick white skin of hate // // until you have to escape to a place /
free from pain

my daughter's studying to be a midwife / we're driving in the car
/ she's talking of university / boys and freshers' week / playing
Ghetto golf with Mya and Zoudecca / talking *de gyal dem* who will
always have her back / driving / we battle for the control of the
radio / *Dad you always listening to Women's Hour* / she hesitates
before she turns the dial / *black women are five times more likely to die
as a result of complications in pregnancy than white women* / we look
at each other / *a black woman discharges herself after being left alone
after loss of blood*

is this where it begins / from adorable mascot for dance troupes & cheerleading / in the turning of your womanhood / there's this shift / daughter of handstands & cartwheels / you land awkwardly / you're in pain / you tell the teacher & you're told to walk it off / you're in pain / you limp to the rest room / nurse tells you it's only a sprain with limited sympathy / you're in pain / they reluctantly call the ambulance & parents / lying in hospital / leg plastered and raised / in the silence I tell you *I'm here Nina, I'm here*

Nina Simone will sing in volumes of pain // Black women with black skin / had to be *strong enough to / take the pain inflicted again / and again,* ask all the Aunt Sarahs // Black woman the colour of tan / have learned *hips invite you / to wrap around you / learned / mouth like wine* to seduce you just ask Sweet Thing // She felt the pain of both worlds / skin yellow a bridge between two worlds / Ask all those named Saffronia // *I'm awfully bitter these days* / written in the pores of brown skin / ask all those named Peaches / if Black women don't feel pain

Living by Troubled Waters #2

There's a spectre in my house
He walks right through me
  – Emma-Jean Thackray, 'Spectre'

Our house was often visited by spirits,
waters often found their way into our home.
My mother of sound mind saw things
other people didn't see, her whole body
a divining rod. She who moved gracefully
in the spirit when it poured, danced in the pool,
raised her arms spellbound to the sky as if
she could touch and hold on to the source.

We lived in a semi-detached house on a hill,
water trickled in, leaving trails and watermarks
only my mother noticed and tried to ignore,
smiling when she saw I was watching
as she whispered to the walls as they drooled.
My mother who mellowed by still waters
could not be at peace, and in this nursery
I learned of *duppies and rolling calves,*

of climbing a flight of stairs on hands and knees,
of a boxed room big enough to leave
a memory in a corner, darkness embodied,
moving into the light, stretching forth an arm
and a child flying down a flight of stairs
sitting on a magic carpet shouting *bada, bada.*
We left the house on the top of the hill, always moving
until Mother found serenity in a home by still waters.

I must call her The Mother with the Pearl Earring

I carry her in the inside pocket of my writer's bag.
Her beauty retained in the years of motherhood –
a huff of sheened afro, gloriously black, my mother
with the pearl earring and full lips, holding a nearly smile.

A photo taken in the middle of the day,
against the background of time lost, of doubt,
of questions so many questions in an endless blue
fatherless sky and fountains singing why, why, why?

And yet if I told you that I have not spoken
to the mother who brought me into this world
for seven years since my *life mother* passed away,
what would you think, what would you imagine?

I look at her picture: my mother caught between
a smile and questioning the taking of the photo –
the way we're forever caught in the moments
of life and death, of regrets and choices made.

On the night Malcom X was assassinated Yuri Kochiyama cradles the head of a dying man

"What Yuri demonstrated… what we call the black radical tradition of which Malcolm X is a part, belongs to everyone…" – Angela Davis, Malcolm X Event, Oxford Union.

To all women of all colour who will hold
      the truth, however bloody and fatally wounded
           hands wet, clothes soiled with blood and tears

To all women of all colour who will lean
      into those Black radical spaces in the midst
           of noise and pandemonium, making safe places

To all women of all colour who will hold
      the last words of a dying man in their cupped hands
           grasping every drop, to carry, for others to carry on

To all women of all colour who may not
      be remembered for being there, cradling the head
           of hope in a hailstorm of bullets and confusion

To all women of all colour who stay
      holding on to revolutions in the palm of their hands
           feeding into new narratives, rooted and blossoming truth

In this Clearing, on this Verandah

i.m. Jean 'Binta' Breeze

'Here', she said, 'in this here place, we flesh; flesh that weeps, laughs;
flesh that dances on bare feet in grass. Love it. Love it hard…'
Beloved – Toni Morrison

We laughed and wept in this flesh, in this place
the woman who held my poems, who held me;
allowed me to hold her work of words;
for words to tend the black men – some bruised,
others broken, but all needing to be set free
in the seasons of wellbeing.

She handed herself back to the motherland
into the hands of her mother, sitting on her verandah –
a place of transition, a resting space in the eve of her life.
The mother of *Dub Poetry* making music with Rastas,
with the sea, with herself, *flesh that dances bare feet* in sand.

And when she returned back to England for those short seasons;
Jean held my arm after a performance, *help me eh, mi duck*
escorting her back to her hotel, her breathing begging for air,
her body unable to keep up with her spirit as she laughed hard.
A woman of fire and desire, who loved words and loved them hard.

A place where we can all breathe

after Sonia Sanchez

Sing my beautiful sister
      Sing words of liberation

Let them be a mirror to the stars at night
Let them be a window to the brightness inside

Sing my beautiful sister
      Between the white spaces

      Between the black places
Sing my beautiful sister

Of a beloved people   God's people

Be my civil rights sister
      My non-violent student

Be my Black arts movement artist
My Nation of Islam sister

          Of a beloved people   God's people

Sing my beautiful sister
      Between the white spaces

      Between the black places
Sing my beautiful sister

And let us learn to lean into his breath   her breath   their breath
Learn to lean into each other's breath and breathe as one

Ovid tells us that **Icarus's mouth** as he vanished into the dark ocean *was crying his father's name.*

Brilliant Corners – Nuzhat Bukhari

Taking Flight (I)

after Hew Locke, *Where Lies the Land?* Hales Gallery, London, 2019

The act of possession in Pocomania, Shango, Vodun, is the moment
of return. A flight from destruction into the circle of light.
 – John La Rose, *The Black Experience and the nature of the Black society*

In the Hales, an art gallery of sails pinned to walls,
boats suspend in air. Houses of colonial splendour
hitch up dem skirts and parade on stilts
as if they could walk on water. And heads,

heads adorned with stolen treasures in Empire
and God's name, are woven with symbolic reminders
of *Poco, Shango,* and *Vodun.* I sat in this world
below the bottom of boats and watched a navy sail away,

as if I were a god from the deep, and I heard the voices
of those who flew away home. No more whip, no more
wandering, no more shame, no more sorrow, no more cries
and blood. Blood on decks, blood on backs, blood between legs.

Would you not jump and watch these boats sail away?
As you sink under, into the darkest abyss.

The Ghazal of the Displaced

being on the outside, holding on to hope like a grain
of sand, echoing the voice of our mothers. We are beautiful people

coming out from the shadows, across the borders,
made in the ugliness of others. We are beautiful people

who ran bare, our footprints pooling sorrow
of bondage, torture and terrors. We are beautiful people

who know the thickness of darkness befriended
and loved it, to escape, leaving sweet lovers. We are beautiful people

scarred by the hope of a new place, seeping
with memories of the blood of brothers. We are beautiful people

tired of the images formed before your very eyes, eyelids
heavy with the prejudice of others. We are beautiful people

from the days of Troy, people have been running with the sun
on their back and under the cover of the moonlight. We are beautiful people.

Praise for those who run in the midnight hour

The weeping wall shed no tears for
those on the edge of borders, the divide between you and me
where we find the weary in the shade of blossoming trees.

The church bells did not ring out for
those who travailed, travelled unforgiving seas,
burning sands, haunting forests, to be found on bended knees.

The minaret call for prayer forgot
those running from yesterday's gods and enemies.
They could only run at midnight to avoid tomorrow's tragedies.

Lampedusa

*I know this is risky and that I will probably lose the boat, but the
shipwrecked on board are exhausted, I will bring them to safety.*
Video released by Sea-Watch, *The Guardian*

For the 43 souls waiting
in the port; for *lampas*
the torch, the light
on an island that should
never be hid; for the wall
that should never be raised;
for the door of Europe
that should never be closed.
For the shipwreck of 2013;
for the 350 and more who
perished; for the nameless
that didn't make it; for
the woman found washed
ashore hugging her baby;
for those who still make
the journey; for those
who fall prey to agents
of Charon – sons of the night.
For the fear of persecution;
for the darkness of torture,
wars and more wars, hunger
for a better life; for the shadow
always following the light;
for being *limbus* on the edge;
for boats that taxi those
from the borders of hell;
for 14 days in limbo
the abode of the unwanted;
for Carola Rackete who
saw the light in the shadow

of humanity; for erasing
imagined lines in the sea;
for breaking rules to save
lives. For more safe harbours.
For the saving of lives.
For hope. For the 43 souls
waiting, waiting, waiting.

Rio Grande

after Oscar Alberto Martinez Ramirez and 23-month-old Valeria

A daughter wraps her arms around her father's neck,
head protruding from his shoulder under his t-shirt

like conjoined twins. *My daughter wrapped herself*
around me, after we'd walked for miles, feigned sleep

for those extra metres wrapped around me. They're lying
face down, cushioned in the muddy water, reeds of blanket

surrounds them undisturbed in their sleep. *My daughter*
wrapped herself around me in the pouring rain,

in the belief that she would be safe and warm.
A daughter still holds on to her father, crossing the river

from the Underworld into the American Dream.
My daughter wrapped herself around me,

leg broken from a gymnastic routine we had practised
so many times – I am helpless to take the pain away.

A father lies face down in the marshy banks of the Rio Grande,
helpless as a daughter holds on wrapped in the arms of a new dawn.

Younous Chekkouri

"I'm finally tasting freedom" he says as he gazes toward the
Atlantic Ocean from the broadwalk of his coastal hometown.
Moroccon freed from Guantanamo Slams IS, Reflects on Toture
The Associated Press, February 16th 2016

Here in Safi, Morocco, the place *to spill, to pour,*
Younous floods the Atlantic with tears and memories.
I'm still in Gitmo, he says as he walks around
an ancient cathedral, remembers pages ripped
from his Quran, seeks sanctuary behind a fortress
too small to protect him from soldiers still running
into his dreams brandishing and shooting guns,
beating his genitals. Younous continues along the beach
called the Head of the Snake, the poison of anxiety still lingering
in his body, no cure to be found in pills and therapies.

Here in Safi, Al-Idrisi once called it the *place of regret*
spoke of sailors who sailed to the other side of the Atlantic
only to be lost on some island. Younous got lost in the lies,
the bounty hunt, the tortures that shipwrecked him
on the shores of Guantanamo. *I'm still in Gitmo,* he says
knowing of the ordeal of being seized and blindfolded.
The sailors in the myth travelled back on ships, he flew back
after 14 years, hooded with ear muffs, arms shackled
to his legs – supposedly free. The sailors became legends
returning to the *place of regret*. His is a tale of regret.

Here in Safi, the narrative lingers from day to day
in every corner of his beaten body. A book coloured
with sleep deprivation and Younous at times grips his side
or catches a faltering breath. He'll look across the horizon,
hear the chorus of freedom sung from a flock of birds,
feel the waters crash against the sea walls, taste the spray
from a hundred drops, count the thousand stars at night
and stand an ocean away from a scar on humanity's
collective memory. And yet, he's still in Gitmo.

Pantoum of the 27

Honest to God… we are in British and French waters.
We don't know which one of them is coming to [rescue us]
Shakar Ali, one of the migrants, sending a last audio message to a relative – Rudaw

27 people died in the Channel; unmarked waters
waiting for authorities to make up their minds
as they clung and held on, in cold dark waters,
one by one they let go of each other and the boat,

waiting for authorities to make up their minds.
Ill-fated winds blew them back into French waters
and the boat barely floated as they let go of each other;
many died before the ferry boat picked them out of cold waters.

Ill fate or winds blew them back into French waters
as they cried, *Please God, rescue us! Please God, rescue us.*
Many died as the ferry boat picked them out of cold waters
with hopes to make it to the other side, whatever the sacrifice.

Please God, rescue us! Please God rescue us, could be heard
but Charon was waiting and the gods were aloof to their pleas.
Although they paid the coins to gangsters and traffickers
seventeen men, seven women and three children perished.

Charon was waiting and the gods were aloof to their pleas
and the channel that divides us from those seeking refuge
swallowed seventeen men, seven women and three children
fleeing with their breath and the clothes on their back.

The channel that divides us from those seeking refuge
clinging, holding on to hope in cold dark waters,
fleeing with their breath and the clothes on their back.
These 27 people died in the Channel of unmarked waters.

After a reading from *Dear Refugee* by Amir Darwish

Yet if the screams of the tortured are audible in the poet's room, is not his activity an offence to human suffering – Czesław Miłosz, *The History of Polish Literature*

I heard of a poet brought into a space
words wrung out of him   words
on the wings of sleep deprivation

The poet wanted to die
after they replaced silence
with punctuated sounds

of blows   electric shocks
and the body drowned
a thousand miles from sea

The poet wanted to die
to cease speaking words
the ultimate blasphemy

as blank pages become
soiled with dirt and piss
filled with his bloody calligraphy

Taking flight (II)

after Hew Locke, *Where Lies the Land?*

I see them rise   *the dead* once embellished in sorrow
in the hum of the silence of this gallery

These bushmen   tradesmen and craftsmen
work their bodies into life

Priest   Talisman and Obeah man
unroll and stretch parchments of skin to the skies

Mothers with babies on breast
their heads adorned with heavens light

Women their bodies no longer
a land to plunder but an oasis of dance and song

And men follow   no longer   emaciated
or torn   but strong and renewed

voices booming across waves

                              bodies dancing   an eternal   jamboree

Remembering is... a putting together of **the dismembered past** to make sense of the trauma of the present

– Homi Bhaba, *The Location of Culture*

You are Impossible to Love (Part 2)

*Okomfo Anokye # Yaa Asantewaa # Nanny of the Maroons # Tacky # Cuffee
of Guyana # Macandal # Boukman # Toussaint L'Overture
Sam Sharpe # Bedward # Paul Bogle*

You are impossible to love, stolen across lands and seas, you carry knowledge in the universe of broken bodies, a lost language in the cave of your mouth, memories in the constellations on your back. Your bodies, temples of trauma.

You carry the seeds of rape, you carry the stories of a people, you carry the grief of those that didn't make it, all in one womb, a swollen pregnant diaspora.

# # #

You are impossible to love, bodies of waters that kept afloat, survived a middle passage, bodies of waters that burst on the altars of resistance. You are impossible to love, vessels vying for a better world, you are new wines in an old world unable to change its old ways.

You are darkened, sweetened nectar of the riotous wine, impossible to love, wine pressed in the vat of oppression, if everyone drank of your wine, they would know and feel how impossible it is to be loved.

# # #

It's written in their statutes, a royal decree, *those kinde of people should be sente forth of the land,* impossible to love. You are the forbode, the River Tiber, Thames, Tame *foaming with much blood.* You are the fear *that this country might be rather swamped by people with a different culture.*

You are *menalin, melano, dark*. You are the one drop of blood that generations try to hide. You are the colour of the earth and the night sky. You are *the colour of my true love's hair*. You are the politics found in the layers of your skin.

You are barely considered human, while white is divine – before the encounter of whiteness, you were loved; skin, hair and body, you were loved, you were dearly loved, you were deified.

Sarah Baartman # Mary Seacole # Alexander Bedward # Marcus Garvey # CLR James # Claude McKay # George Padmore # Amy Ashwood Garvey # Claudia Jones # John La Rose # Edward Kamau Brathwaite # Jean 'Binta' Breeze

After **Hew Locke, *Wreck*, 2021**

Siting on the quayside
watching boats come
and leave, trade winds
that brought our fathers
from another land. Trade winds
so treacherous, so dangerous.
A trade of stories for the winds
that swirl around our minds.

Our fathers, our mothers,
culled from a land soaked in blood
lulled by the lie for a better life
are wrecked on a far distant shore.

In the hull of our existence
we carry the bones of our fathers
as spirits walk along the boards
and leave their footsteps behind.

From an early age, an artist
from the school of schooners
has seen these footsteps others
have missed, caught up
in the trade winds from Guyana
to Edinburgh – a cold place –
from Edinburgh to Guyana
in time for Independence.

An artist accustomed
to the winds of the sea
will make boats, hundreds
of boats, to carry ornaments
of being, trinkets of memories,

ferrying the souls of yesterday
and today, a votive reminder
that we're all floating
on the same ocean.

And this wreck
will imagine beyond borders
beyond shores, beyond hate
bearing hope and carrying the dreams
of a young man sitting on the quayside
watching boats come and leave.

Black Square

after Kazimir Malevich, *Black Square*, 1915

In the year 1913, trying desperately to free art from the dead weight
of the real world, I took refuge in the form of the square.
  – Kazimir Malevich, *Non-Objective World* (1927)

They say this was the drawing of a new age
an escape from reality   a refuge found in a
black square Oh! For black squares to appear
& disappear in extreme moments   to wait to
inhabit those difficult places   to give voice
to things unsaid   to be found in a safe place
where the pain of a past folds into itself over
& over & over   until black squares feed on
the fears of you & me   I want black squares
to swallow whole   the haunting white ball
in *The Prisoner* that follows you   I desire
black squares when times of being Black is
more than I can bear   like   *The Battle of Negroes in a dark cave*   found
inscribed   under Malevich's *Black Square*
a racist joke   in response to French writer
Alphonse Allais' caption   *Negroes fighting*
in a Cellar at Night this eternal tragicomedy
is no joke   we're always fighting   fighting
for the right to breathe &when that's gone
fighting for justice & justness in a square ring
gloved tears becoming jabs of coiled-up anger
to exist another day for our sons & daughters
fighting to be heard   fighting for our stories
to be told until you see JUST US until there's
justice until there's love under a black square

Cain rose against Abel

NEGROES CONFINED *in the* CAGE

—

[Bridge-Town, Jan. 13, 1818]

To border on our humanity
these 'cavea' hollow places of morality –

Negroes' Names	*Owners' Names.*
Ned Robin	Mr. Gibbs
Phillis	Isaac Roach
Cobah	Kelsay's Estate (Own. unkn.)
George	Captain Adams
James Mings	Mr. Benj. Bostock

Am I my brother's keeper
or am I the cage keeper?

| *Frankey* . . . . | Richard Wells |
| *Thomas* . . . . | Mr. Henry Perkins |

Owners of Runaway Slaves are requested to send to
this place of confinement at least once a week,
when such as have been lodged here can be delivered to the. – By order,

J. SIDNEY, *Cage-keeper.*

Abel's blood cries from the ground

NEGROES CONFINED *in the* CAGE

[Bridge-Town, Feb. 21, 1818]

What have you done? Listen –
your brother's blood cries out to me
from the soil, from the sea
from the river, from the silhouette of trees –

Negroes' Names	Owners' Names.
Ned Robin	Mr. John Gibbs (decd.)
George	Captain Adams
John William	Mr. Patrick Ward
Thomas	Mr. Henry Perkins
James Mings	Mr. Benj. Bostock

Cursed shall you be by the soil that gaped
with its mouth to take your brother's blood
Mr John Gibbs (deceased) in Dante's seventh circle.

Owners of Runaway Slaves ████████████ to
this place █ confine███ at least once a week,
████████████████████
███████████████
████████████████████

Abel, Hebel breath be they name

NEGROES CONFINED *in the* CAGE

—

[Bridge-Town, May 9, 1818]

Negroes' Names	Owners' Names.
James Mings	Mr. Benj. Bostock
Tom	Mr. Robert Wotherspoon
Frederick	Mr. Harding

James Mings, have you escaped,
seen the cycles of the three moons
dipped in the river, running free.

John	Mrs. C. Barnes, Antigua
Henry	Mr. Henry Thorp
Grigg	Mrs. Hetty Toppin (widow)
Peter	Mr. John Carew
Kitty Ann	Mr. Thomas Pollard
Mandeville	Mr. John Young
John Wilcher	Mrs. Eliz. Reece
Mimbo	Miss Elizabeth Ower
Nanny	Miss Elizabeth Niles

'...and to the sprinkled blood that speaks
a better word than the blood of Abel.'
  The blood of the enslaved.

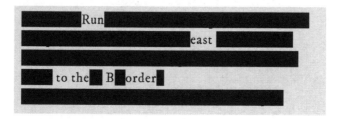

Run

east

to the B order

Living by Troubled Waters #3

For you there might be a brighter star… For you there might be another song
Stevie Wonder – 'Another Star' from *Songs in the Key of Life*

Black bodies as bright as the night star
are being put out, extinguished,
sacrificed on the altar of whiteness,
crying out *I can't breathe.*

I pray as I watch the skies at night;
they become the comets, asteroids
finding their own trajectory,
never dying but lighting up the night.

Those things they never attained here –
other galaxies and nebulae
will hold their brightness,
emanate light, years from now.

I want stars to be named after
George, Breonna, Ahmaud
Philando, Eric, and Trayvon
Cherry, Mark, and Rashan.

Stars that will illuminate
other civilisations: where
skin is touched for its beauty
and not curiosity; where hair

black and wooly has its own
allure; where walking at night
under bright stars is not dwarfed
by the red and blue lights of patrol cars;

where language is not a border to be
crossed; where comeliness is not coloured
in shades of lightness; where full lips
are not commodified; where god
walks in the skin of Blackness
and whatever colour she desires.

Black Pietas

After Renée Cox, *Yo Mamma's Pieta* (1994)

From
the heavens.
The hulls of ships, the seabed,
cotton fields, between sugar cane.
From the cage where you're chained.
Hanging from blossoming trees,
from *white only* entrances,
from freedom buses,
from church on a Sunday,
midweek prayer meetings,
from jogging, from shopping,
from sleeping in beds,
from the hull of our own cars.
These Black Pietas.

The body
these dark-skinned divinities
doing their father's business,
never making it home
for supper.

The mother
how she must have pleaded,
begged for his body, the body
she brought into this world;
the blood that stained her face
at the foot of the cross, before
hard hands, cruel hands, led
her away. But she will wait
for the body to be returned
and hold the child fully
grown, fully dead in her
outstretched arms and
know the heavy,
weight of grief.

We Were Already Divine

If we were made in his image
Then call us by our names
  – Erykah Badu, *On & On*

The evening meal was in progress… Jesus knew that the Father had put all things
under his power, and that he had come from God and was returning to God.
  – St John 13:2,3 NIV

In another gospel, in a remote country cottage, a well-timed retreat
for Black men. The table is coloured with more than bread and wine;
here a bowl of ackee & saltfish, there rice & peas, chickens (stewed,
southern fried, or for the adventurous, jerk seasoned). On another table
curry goat & white rice, flanked by side dishes; dumpling,
plantain, roast breadfruit, sweet potato and to finish the evening
gizzada, grater cakes, sweet potato pudding and rum cake.
Our last supper before we went back to trouble and trials
of Black men too outspoken, false tribunals and another season
working in the belly of the beast. We sons of gods, with locks adorned,
some unwrapped, others with afro-picked haloes, softened glorious crowns
and baldheads anointed with olive oil. We sons of gods in the presence
of Black ancestors on white walls and with the help of some *Baduizm*
shared the bread of our history and drank the deep wine of Blackness.

After reading 'To Toussaint L'Overture' by Wordsworth, Ira Aldridge is often visited by his Spirit

And did I not know
Toussaint – the most unhappy of men! –

The story which lived within your bones lived with
In mine from day to day as I walked this unpleasant land.

Oh, miserable Chieftain,
Your sorrow filled my very veins.

Often times upon the stage, I have felt
Alone in some deep dungeon's earless den

I've learned through savage critique
To *wear rather in thy bonds a cheerful brow.*

And I can only hope to have left footprints, as you have,
In this ever-changing sand; *Power that will work*

For thee – air, earth and skies – for all those that follow;
Of whatever hue of humanity they may assume

Believing that hate will be starved in the shadows
Of bright hope *and love, and man's unconquerable mind.*

To the Public making his appearance as Othello
if he should have the PRESUMPTION to appear,
he is **Threatened with DAMNATION**
his skin too dark to personate the
'DUSKY MOOR'

I am Ira Frederick Aldridge;
"A child of the sun, black my countenance,
yet I stand before you in the light of my soul."

If Only We Could Walk On Air

JUST ANOTHER KID

14 years old and 6ft
shoulders of Atlas carrying the world.
He carried the absence of his father
in jail and out of jail
carried the reputation of a family
carried a mother who was carrying
her own problems; a baby on the way,
whilst another child aged nine
excluded for carrying a knife.

So, he squeezed his size on a sofa at night
and spread his length all day on the streets.

Some days if you waited long enough
in the midst of quietness and no audience
you see the child carrying the teenager,
putting him down for a while, running free.

RADIO RAHEEM

After the killing of his radio
in the film *Do The Right Thing*
Raheem is caught up in a malestorm,
spits and splutters, body pulled by
three police officers, their limbs
like branches trail around him
and lift him off his feet, choke-hold,
holding him suspended, long after;
Gary that's enough, Gary that's enough
for a moment Raheem, walks on air
in the burning heat of the night.

ATLAS

If this young man entered smiling
the odds where in our favour.
New Nikes, new jacket
and he's alive and buzzing.
In an exclusion centre,
in a one-to-one session
I'm trying to break things down
as we watch *Do The Right Thing*.
He says, *Nah, I ain't got time for this.*

WALKING ON AIR

Everyone is walking on eggshells
slipping through doors moulding into the walls –
a storm is brewing and before I know it
I'm holding Young Atlas after an argument with one
of the other lads, who dared to laugh at him.
Pride buckles, his world slips from his shoulders;
fucking move out the way. I pray and hope
I can bring him down, pleading with the gods
that made him. *For fucksake I'm begging you, move.*
Young Atlas takes a hold of me and throws me
against the door; the glass panel breaks like a fault line.
He's beyond the horizon of reason.
Listen to me.
I'd like to say he heard, remembered every lesson
of life I shared with him. But he's gone – a physical
attack on a teacher and violent assault on a student –
and now he slips into a future that won't hold him so reverently.

I'm holding a scream

To make someone wait the constant prerogative of all power,
'age-old' pastime of humanity.
   – Roland Barthes

The scream resonates within this body,
my body contorts to hold the scream.
Edvard Munch knew the scream under
swirling red skies and there's no bridge
stable enough to take me across these
troubled waters and I can't wait
for a parting of the seas, the oceans
that already hold the liquid screams
of my ancestors; waiting for a god
who would have my people cornered
on this dreadful earth for centuries
and centuries by a belief that hunts
us from behind and holds us hostage
to a sea of white supremacy.

You see all that the white has made us suffer –

in the sacrifice of bodies on the frontline
of an epidemic; in the call of a fiery
Windrush; in the screams of burning bodies
of Grenfell; in the borders raised against
Black and Brown bodies, leaving them
to drown in cold dark waters;

The white man's god ask him to commit crimes –

these acts of negligence ignore the cries
of a people that say it's not safe, the cries
of a people who say they want change,
leaving souls to chose to swim or fly
before they die.

I'd resurrect the ancestors that stood that night
on the shores of Haiti, call on Boukman to
pray, call him to remind us of gods that will
hear the lament of Black voices, will
understand the sacrifice of Black bodies
understand the earth that reached up
for those that flew
or hung from low bearing trees –

...throw away the image of the white men's god who is so pitiless.
Listen to the voice for liberty that speaks in all our hearts.

Toussaint

ment in the Island of St. Domingo, was calculated to give much alarm to those in this country who are interested in West-India property. Toussaint's republic was viewed as a formidable example, and its effects might have spread to the whole circle of islands where negroes are found. ...saint only recognizes a no- ...on France. His children ...is obliged to temporize. ...f views, in which the wishes ...the dictates of Bonaparte's ...believed that Toussaint will ...feel that he is not indepen- ...A great number of French ...it to St. Domingo to assert ...French republic. If necessary, the French government is to be allowed to charter to the number of seventy English vessels to carry out the troops without delay, because it may be of great importance to execute the plan before Toussaint has the least intimation of peace being concluded between France and England, and of course before he can be prepared to assert his independence against such a force as will be sent. It is added, that Martinique is to remain in our hands, for a time, as a pledge that Bonaparte will execute this purpose faithfully.

In Toussaint's constitution there is a clause which permits the introduction of new cultivators, that is, either new negroes, for the encouragement of agriculture, or run-away negroes from the other colonies. In the one case, the slave trade is to be carried on by negroes; in the other, all the slaves already in the West Indies are to be free on reaching St. Domingo!

You are Impossible to Love (Part 3)

Eric Garner # Michael Brown # Tamir Rice # Breonna Taylor # George Floyd # 9 African Americans killed in Charleston during a Bible study # 4 American Asians killed in Atlanta at local spas # 22 people killed in Texas # 11 Jewish Americans killed at the Tree of Life Synagogue Pittsburgh # 10 people killed whilst shopping in Buffalo, New York

You are angry for every George Floyd that cries for their mother. You are angry for every Breonna Taylor murdered in their doorway.

You are angry for your father wearing the mask, on the foundry floor, in shops, on buses, saying nothing to *nigger* hurled at him; you wanted him to take it off, and let loose.

You cringe to hear my best friends are like you; You balk at the idea that they don't see your colour;

You are the tales they tell their children, Caliban, the wild man, the boogey man, the uncivilised.

You are the descendant of Ham cursed by God for looking at the nakedness of your father, you are the lowest register on the hierarchy of colours, you are the skulls too large, you are cocks and vaginas that swing and open wide.

You are the gunned, stifled, chased, beaten, killed for drawing on air from pockets of lungs in an already deflated body.

You must be impossible to love, when they murder you over and over again; when royalty and government leaders stifle on the word *sorry* for the Black holocaust of the enslaved.

David Oluwale # Christopher Alder # Sean Rigg # Kingsley Burrell # Stephen Lawrence # Mark Duggan # Dalian Atkinson # Rashan Charles # Nicole Smallman & Bibaa Henry # 27 People died in the crossing of the English Channel # Girl Q # Shireen Abu Aqleh

When warm weather came, Baby Suggs, holy, followed by every black man, woman, and child who could make it through, took her great heart to **the Clearing**

– Toni Morrison, *Beloved*

Laying of Hands

MAN-TO-MAN

Hands on his back, let him know you're there,
he leans into you, he moves off you, he signals
for the ball, *'I'm gonna take you downtown.'*
He gets the ball, he shimmies to one side, you hold
the lane, he comes into you, you lay your hands on him.

He backs off you, crossovers and fakes, the ball
between the legs to go one way but you know him,
as if you were gods who had played with the moons
of Jupiter – the ball behind the back to go the other way.
He's got the lane; he's got the drive.

Now it's on; body-to-body contact, the press
of flesh, the exchange of sweat, the alignment
of planets both pull into each other's momentum;
defying gravity, bodies arch in celestial flight.
The ball hits the ring and we both fall to earth.

AFTER A BASKETBALL GAME

She takes off your top, lays her hand on you,
pushes you against the wall, while Janet Jackson sings
any time, and any place she kneels before you, tongue
leaving a trail of intentions down your torso, her mouth open
for holy communion, to take of your body, to take it all.

Skirt around my waist / wall against my face you're
hands find the small of her waist, fingers still wet,
her body varnished with sweat, saliva and sweet kisses,
and she speaks your name and you're speaking in tongues,
while bodies shiver, you press her against the wall, holding her

as a goddess. *I'm not gonna stop no, no, no,* knowing
if you release each other, the night would come and you would
disappear and whatever blessings you have for each other
will dissipate in the darkness so you push deeper, you hold
tighter and together, you make hymns, rising to the heavens.

AFTER AN EVENING OF LOVING

Body sweating, heavy breathing, I slip into the back pews,
praying nobody notices. *Can a man hide in secret places*
where I cannot see him? the preacher warns, his hands
lifts to the heavens – the same hands raised to beat me,
but Mother's hand softly on his shoulder held him back.

Do I not fill the heavens and the earth? My father's hands
that know the soil of the Black Country. A father that lives
by the codes of almanacs, waits for new moons to rise
before new seeds were planted. Planting seeds of hope
in people living in a strange land, *Come unto me*

all that labour and I will give you rest, and before I know it
I'm praying, I'm falling on the floor, I'm being touched
by the spirit, hands raised, body bucking, becoming a vessel
of emotions overflowing; after, we hold each other,
laying hands on one another in a flood of praise and song.

The Act of Remembering

Now that I, your Lord and Teacher, have washed
your feet, you should also wash one another's feet.
St John 13:14 NIV

We took off our brogues, leathers
and crocodile skins, folded our silk socks
whilst others with their Clarks and cotton socks
waited, waited for eyes to be distracted by sisters
in white, singing *meet me by the river, some day.*

Old men who knew rivers,
waited for the pouring of water
in enamel basins, waited for the pouring
of the spirit, hands clapping, backs arched,
the jerk, the side drop, the top torso waving
in an imaginary wind, blowing through the aisles.

We jostled to wash our best friends' feet,
avoided the hard-skinned, corn-heavy,
decade-stained feet of old men,
                              but the old souls
knew the game, broke the line, changed seating.
Wrapped white towels around our waists,
singing, *when my Lord shall call me home*
happy, happy home beyond the skies

our white shirt sleeves rolled up;
silk ties tucked away;
we kneeled before elders,
scooped handfuls of water,
washed weary feet,
leaving a bowl filled
with a cloud of witness.

The Suit

The making of a man

He never said the suit made the man
but he wore suits with pride; when
the car broke down, which happened
numerous times, he'd back off his jacket
roll up his sleeves, tinker and tat
under the bonnet, draw out
a white handkerchief and surrender
as he cleaned his hands, put on his jacket –
Son, we're walking; walking miles in his suit.

Or when he shuffled down a flight of stairs
Early in the morning on his bottom, rubbing
the grit-grinding pain out of his knees
before he could straighten up, put on his suit
to make his way to work, to a foundry of iron,
fire and dirt, black soot everywhere,
wearing overalls in the heat
but in the cool of the evening
return home wearing his suit.

He saved the best for Sundays and conventions,
tie held straight with a gold slide; shirt ironed
and always holding a briefcase and an umbrella
like Steed from *The Avengers* carrying the word
of God. He never said the suit made the man
but he wore suits with pride.

First Suit

Burton's, Dudley, that first suit itched
with a sheep's revenge, reluctant to be shorn,
separated from his coat. A suit heavy with
pure new wool for a ten-year-old. For a wedding.
A child who wanted something lighter, something better,
moaned all day. A mother who had to budget,
spent most of her money on her child; with what was left
she bought a dress pattern and two yards of plain cotton
from a market stall, spent all night stitching.

Finding my father in the field of words

My father who could read the skies at night
and taught himself to play the accordion
struggled with words I could read aloud.

My mother of many words, shared words
through psalms and proverbs, would shepherd
him through pastures of words and wait for him

to turn sounds in the space of his mouth
and traced letters across the page
until they formed a phrase he understood.

A father who watched bricklayers, plasterers; read
between the lines of spirit levels and converted
an outside loo to the back of the house.

Would pull spark plugs out of car engines,
dismantle a watch and any other moving object
and put them back again, to begin again

but struggled to put words together
to make an engine purr out of stories
and travel confidently wherever he wanted.

He asked a teenager to guide him through his labyrinth,
to be patient when he lost his place, standing face to face
with the beast that would stand in his way.

An impatient teenager with his father, one late evening
reading a word at a time, too slowly for a young man
who had just read a Harper Lee classic in the day,
who tutted and forgot *it's a sin to kill a mocking bird.*

after duckanoos...

after the hostilities between father and son
after the amnesty brokered in the absence
of a mother leaving on holiday for Jamaica,
pleading *the two of you must look after each other,*

after duckanoos; cornmeal and gratered coconut,
sweetened with brown sugar, spiced cinnamon, salt,
nutmeg, and vanilla, mixed in a bowl with a wooden
spoon until thick but not wet, warning from my father,
that cornmeal always swells when it meets water
and maybe there was a proverb... spoonful the size
of a lemon placed in the middle of foiled paper,
here my father tenderly parcelled and tied
with a tenderness I wasn't so often accustomed to
and immersed in boiling water. Hand on my shoulder
he enfolds me with tales of young men, banana-leaved
packages boiled in pots left by river banks or beaches
as they dived into waters or played makeshift cricket,
to return, to untie and bite, their rich rough essence
dissolving sweetness under a setting cornmeal sun.

Amulet

To ward off evil spirits, indigo blue is added to the bath, and the forehead marked with
a blue cross... the midwife offers a prayer before bringing the baby out in the air.
– Edward Kamau Braithwaite, *Folk Culture of the Slaves in Jamaica*

My mother slipped the Lord's Prayer
into my satchel on my way to school,

or was it the handkerchief she folded neatly
into my inside suit pocket on Sundays, or

the olive oil she ritually rubbed into my skin,
a daily sacrament, to anoint my holy body

that others would demonise or terrorise –
Vaseline for dried lips to keep me

from evil, the *Reckitt's Blue* she slipped in the washing,
for white only; for the lamb that would be preyed upon.

Space in the Front Room

...and when he seeth the blood upon the lintel, and on the
two side posts, the lord will pass over the door. Exodus 12.23 KJV

The Angels

We never knew that blood had been shed on the streets, in the factories, as parents daubed the frame of their houses with their own blood-shed. Blood in the mortar of houses that barely stood, the frozen pane of glass in the morning, the breath that went before us before we rose out of bed.

Only for young men to inherit these stories, the retelling of hell on earth, but there was a deliverance from trouble and trial; a space in the front room, in the shubeens, that transformed into another world for that evening, far from the boot-stomping, voice-baying terror of Thatcher's England.

From the moment we got the invite, heard the whisper on the grapevine, *there's a blues tonight at Marse Joes,* or *Cynthia's mum is holding a birthday party* – we got a ticket to fly. And so, we count down the days, unemployed, college, or on apprenticeships waiting for the moment of feeling whole.

We dressed to kill after being told we were nothing or less than, saved up money, or dropped pardner for that suit we bought from Reiss Menswear. We sought after Pierre Cardin shoes, jumpers and shirts we wore for church conventions but sneaked out the house late at night looking like we stepped off a set.

And those brothers who were *hearticle*, wearing dreads under those big leather hats or tams; rocked up in Gabicci polos, Farah suede cardigans, pork-pie hats; others denim trousers, sewn-in front-and back-crease, Clarks shoes, army combats and matching shirts, always with gold chains and gold rings if you could afford it.

And then those bass speakers, amps wired up, primed for take-off, that when the right sound *licked* that bass, like *Promised Land*, you felt it in your chest to the tips of your wings. The horns section got you ready to fly, followed by the call the *wohoi, well now* and Dennis Brown led the way through Wasmara, Addis Ababa and Shashamane land whilst *we're riding on the King's Highway*.

You knew for that moment Dennis Brown was Moses and Aswad the prophets and we knew *The reality of our true being and levity* and we had left this earth, with our eyes closed, heads rocking, the body walking and prancing on air. And angels were watching over us during those troubled times.

Man and Woman

And then those bass speakers, amps wired up, primed for take-off, that when the right sound *licked* that bass, you were under a rocket, beginning its launch sequence to take us out this world making the *Thunderbird* vibrate in the cups.

But on other occasions the atmosphere, the altitude changed, the moment you were waiting for when the music changed, Lovers' Rock…
> *shal lah lah lah lah, lah, lah, lah lah;*
> *shal lah lah lah lah lah lah lah laaah*

and then the skip in the beat and Jean Adebambo begins her ode to *Paradise* and by now if you haven't come with a lover, you find a willing stranger in this church of sensuality, this space of humanity, on the dance floor.

You pulled her in closer with her arms wrapped around your neck; you both merged into each other and nothing was forbidden and you believed Jean for a short moment when she said *You make my life such a paradise / you make it so real to me*.

Account of the final abolition of SLA-
VERY in ENGLAND.
*(From Clarkson's history of the Abolition of
the Slave Trade.)*

Before the year 1700, planters, merchants, and others, resident in the West Indies, but coming to England, were accustomed to bring with them certain slaves to act as servants with them during their stay. The latter, seeing the freedom and the happiness of servants in this country, and considering what would be their own hard fate on their return to the islands, frequently absconded. Their masters of course made search after them, and often had them seized and carried away by force. It was, however, throw out by many on these occasions, that the English laws did not sanction such proceedings, for that all persons who were baptized became free. The consequence of this was, that most of the slaves, who came over with their masters, prevailed upon some pious clergyman to baptize them. They took of course godfathers of such citizens as had the generosity to espouse their cause. — When they were seized they usually sent to these, if they had an opportunity, for their protection. And in the result, their godfathers, maintaining that they had been baptized, and that they were free on this account as well as by the general tenor of the laws of England, dared those, who had taken possession of them, to send them out of the kingdom.

The planters, merchants, and others, being thus circumstanced, knew not what to do. They were afraid of taking their slaves away by force, and they were equally afraid of bringing any of the case before a public court. In this dilemma, in 1729, they applied to York and Talbot, the attorney and solicitor-general for the time being, and obtained the following strange opinion from them :-

" We are of opinion, that a slave by coming from the West Indies into Great Britain or Ireland, either with or without his master, does not become free, and that his master's right and property in him is not thereby determined or varied, and that baptizm doth not bestow freedom on him nor make any alteration in his temporal condition in these kingdoms. We are also of opinion, that the master may legally compel him to return again to the plantations."

This cruel and illegal opinion was delivered in the year 1729. The planters, merchants and others, gave it of course all the publicity in their power. And the consequences were as might easily have been apprehended. In a little time slaves absconding were advertised in the London papers as runaways, and rewards offered for the apprehension of them, in the same brutal manner as we find them advertized in the land of slavery. They were advertised also in the same papers, to be sold by auction, sometimes by themselves, and at others with horses, chaises and harness. They were seized also by their masters or by persons employed by them, in the very streets, and dragged from thence to the ships; and so unprotected now were these poor slaves, that persons in nowise concerned with them began to institute a trade in their persons, making agreements with captains of ships going to the West Indies to put them on board at a certain price. This last instance shows how far human nature is capable of going, and is an answer to those persons who have denied that kidnapping in Africa was a source of supplying the slave-trade. It shows, as all history does from the time of Joseph, that, where there is a market for the persons of human beings, all kinds of enormities will be practised to obtain them.

These circumstances, then, as I observed

The Fields of Bilston College

after Warrior Charge – Aswad

Where young Black men gathered around a fire of sounds crackling
from ghetto blasters, we warmed on an already-hot summer's day.
We were the young thunder and lightning, sparking
in an oncoming storm we never knew was coming – how
would we? We were gods already firing lightning bolts, forging
identities, we held on to the fire burning in *Warrior Charge*, the bass,
vibrating *Du-du-dum, du-du-dum, du-du-dum, du-du-dum.*

The drum intro you'll never forget and the sax, chanting on the top
of percussion, and the bass holding up the song like Ashanti warriors
and the synthesizer's intermittent unmistakeable *puh, puh* sound
and the harmonica wail, wailing the cry of the unheard –
but when that bass came back, we were lost, legs up, arms flying
and heads swaying, heads bowing, heads flailing back with locks
of hair cutting through the air, the summer burning air, with revolutions.

Living by Troubled Waters #4

A stone's-throw away from *The Fields,*
across an avenue behind houses at the end
of the lane where the grass was wilder,
the terrain more rugged and tracks
were known only to the adventurous,
to where a Black family
owned a detached house, a mother
who was sweet as the grater cake
she gave me and rough as its texture
on sad days when her husband worked
long shifts, a son named Danny who taught me
to run on the ball of my feet and not flat-footed
and a daughter named Tina, older than me,
who smiled, leaving me enchanted;
these are the tracks that led us to waters
where we were botanists in the springtime
making sense of wiggling exclamations,
tadpoles inquisitive as us in their world
as in the palm of our hands; jumping
from rock to rock, we who would dare
to leap across the rapids and after
we would crawl through reeds,
hide in the bank and throw dirt bombs
on enemies advancing, enemies
we shared sweets with, dipping lollipops
and liquorice into sherbet-coloured evenings;
these are the waters that cut through wild lands
that bordered homes, the GKN works,
and the football field; these are the short cuts
for running to school or picking up *pardners,*
these are the walks with Tina, two years older,
who still followed you into wet dreams; this
is the story of the man who carried the whole
world in a shopping trolley, who disappeared

after we found his trolley in the river; this is
the evening I finished school late and had to take
the short cut in the dark before Dad got home,
realising *nigger* thrown at you from
an older group of school kids made you
remember how to run on the pads
of your feet, ran a mile without stopping
and never looked back. These are the waters
we got lost in the making of our youth.

We, the Brothers of the Salute

This passing of Black brothers on escalators
in a crowded room or a busy promenade

at traffic lights, at night clubs and churches
in the country, the shibboleth in a strange land.

The first time you notice a brother; the gaze,
the meeting of the eyes, Black knights of the realm

raising our heads slightly (never our visors),
always the nod to show friendly intentions

in a hostile environment
and continue our way.

You left in between the snowdrops that fell lightly

In a world of floppy-disks and hard drives, with Christmas
around the corner. I get a phone call, 'you need to come to the hospital.'

The day before, you were supposed to be coming home,
you heard my mother struggle to move you from bed to chair;

a practice run for what life would be, moving your stroke-hit body
like a mighty oak; you were leaning, heavy, struck by lightning.

I see mum at the entrance of the ward, *Roy, daddy gone, daddy gone.*
I hold mum to the mumbling of nurses and I'm trying to compute.

And there you are behind a closed curtain, unbelievably still.
So, you gone old man, you really gone, I touch your chest

something solid about your chest, something absolute,
the lack of movement and I know you're not coming back.

I make a pillow of your chest and lie there; tears trickle
on to this rock. It's only been an hour since they called me

warmth still resides in you like in the morning; the heat left over
from the coal fire you made the evening before, fires I'll have to make.

Mum stirs me, *Roy I was here all the time, I only popped out,*
I come back and im head lean, mout open, mi touch him and he head…

I'm holding my mum as she cries, bawls, she who never left your side,
imagines she has failed you, but you knew what you were doing.

Outside, Christmas draws near, and time falls
lightly like snow as the world programs itself for celebrations.

Praise for My Father

Birds flying high… Sun in the sky
– Nina Simone, 'Feeling Good' from *I Put a Spell On You*

In praise of Ishmael Zechariah,
my father with the names of prophets.
In praise of pockets full of Bounty
when you came back from work;

In praise of the coconuts you held
with a slight bend in the arm, the way
your machete kissed the shell and it opened,
the way we leaned our heads back and drank;

In praise of the moon and North star
you navigated for seasons of growing
and finding our way back home; In praise
of the spirit of the Maroons from St Thomas

always looking for a way back to Africa;
In praise of almanacs you read religiously
with the help of mother; In praise of razor blades
and the splash of Old Spice on your face.

In praise of big old Bibles that propped the family up;
In praise of accordions and mouth organs you played
singing *this world is not my home, I'm only passing through.*
If heaven was not my home, Dear Lord what would I do.

In praise of a higher being but I won't give him blue eyes;
In praise of wrestling, Big Daddy and Giant Haystacks;
In praise of the day I was taller than you, wrestled you,
found myself on my back, knee in my solar plexus

and a warning *So, you think you is man;* In praise
of johnny cakes – fried dumplings the size of flying saucers –
taking us out of this world, full of butter, golden as the sun;
In praise of those times you pulled me back from the sun;

In praise of *butterflies all havin' fun, you know what I mean.*
Sleep in peace when day is done, that's what I mean.
In praise of Bounty – bookshelves
filled with encyclopaedias a volume for every week;

In praise of the mothership of your dreams
a universe of words, safe havens and clearings;
In praise of the average life we lived
so others could have a beginning;

In praise of open doors for every tongue to enter; In praise
of the mantra to serve others; In praise of your vision
for making a better life for a fatherless child; In praise of love
you smothered my mother with like butter on hot johnny cakes;

In praise of the words I'm sending you across the galaxy,
words of love; In praise of that better place you're in;
In praise *of rivers running free,* in praise *of freedom*
in praise of *feeling good, you know what I mean.*

To be free

The Subscriber offers a reward of Eight Dollars to any person who will apprehend his Servant named George, who absented himself on Wednesday the 20th last. He is a short Black Man, a native of this Island, and has many relations in Bridge Town.
reward of £20 to any person who can prove her being harboured by any white or free person (for 20

ABSCONDED from the subscriber, on the 8th of July, 1814, two Barbadian MEN (brothers), by name Pompey and Anthony – the former a black man, the later a tawney-skin, lately the property of my brother. Thomas G. Armstrong, deceased. – A reward of in Bridge-Town, be given to any person or persons for reward of £20 to any person who can prove her being harboured by any white or free person (for 20 scriber, living in the Parish of St. Phillip

July 30 – 3a.   JOS. ARMSTRONG

ABSENTED from the service of the Subscriber on the 28th March last, a Negro Woman named Philida, about 45 years old, 5 feet high, black-skin, large eye lines, much marked with small pox, and splay-footed; she formerly belonged to Henry E Holder Esq Joes' River, where she has a son, and may probably be concealed there, or in that neighbourhood. She was last the property of Henry Parkinson, Esq. deceased, and had a husband at Clapham Plantation, where she has formerly been taken from. A reward of Eight Dollars will be paid for apprehending her, and a further reward of £20 to any person who can prove her being harboured by any white or free person (for 20 days) able to pay the penalty incurred, as the Law will positively be enforced against any person so offending.

July 30 – 3a.   JOHN DEAR

{   }

To the Heron who stood with me
in the ruins of another Black man's life

after Gwendolyn Brooks & Gil Scott-Heron

To the Heron long and lean standing still on the corners
where the waters bend; to the Heron gracefully grey
poised at the water's edge; to the Heron painted
in the tapestry of reeds, waiting, waiting – I want
to learn the art of waiting in these *dread*-full times,
thick engulfing, choking times; to the Heron
long-limbed, taking one, two steps, stretching
those wings, leaping like Jordon – *to rise*
in brilliance; to all Herons from the lineage
of Bennu *He who came into being by himself.*

To all the Herons left school, real cool;
to the Heron lurking late in summertime;
to the Heron with the slow wing beats
of a double-bass on a Jazz June evening;
to the Heron motionless, still standing still;
to Gil Scott-Heron whilst I'm here *standing*
in the ruins of another Black man's life... I am Death
cried the Vulture for the people of the light, yet, here
we stand on the muddy banks alive, longing for change;
to all those gliding towards the sunset, beautiful is your name.

Notes

The names found in 'You are Impossible to Love' are some of the **Windrush generation,** wrongly detained, deported, and denied legal rights, as mentioned in the following article from *The Guardian*. https://www.theguardian.com/uk-news/2018/apr/20/its-inhumane-the-windrush-victims-who-have-lost-jobs-homes-and-loved-ones

'An aubade in response to how do you feel...' was written in response to George Floyd's brutal murder by a policer officer named Derek Chauvin on 25th May 2020. Viewed across the globe from internet to front rooms, we watched a modern-day lynching of a black man crying *I can't breathe* for nearly nine minutes.

Mother from her Child: original image from *The American Anti-slavery Almanac* (1840), The New York Public Library: 'Selling a mother from her child'. NYPL Digital Collections. https://digitalcollections.nypl.org/

'Visitation of the Spirits' are a collection of stories from my mother passed down to me in the traditions of the griot, news reports without dates but often associated to great disasters and major events, dates verified by newspaper research. I also wanted to look at the thin line between spirituality and what others might see as mental illness.

'Nanny of the Black Country wearing Converse All Stars' Pocomania or Pukkumina (possibly from Spanish, 'a little madness'). Afro-Jamaican cults descended from surviving forms of African religion mixed with Protestant elements from the time of the Great Revival in Jamaica in 1860–2. *Oxford University Press.* Obeah (sometimes spelled Obi, Obeya, or Obia) is a system of spiritual healing and justice-making practices developed among enslaved West Africans in the West Indies (*Wikipedia*). In Jamaica, the indigenous people who once inhabited the island, the Tainos, named the island "Xaymaca", meaning "land of wood and water". (*VisitJamaica.*)

'Mothers of Love' was influenced by watching Ballet Black *Then or Now* by William Tucket, partly choreographed around *Sending Love* by Adrienne Rich, many thanks to Director of Poetry Fiona L. Bennett.

After watching https://www.youtube.com/watch?v=uFYWNUXNPRc Angela Davis inspired me to write **'On the night Malcom X was assassinated Yuri Kochiyama…'**.

'Taking Flight (I)&(II)' was influenced by Hew Locke's *Where Lies the Land?* His work often interrogating the languages of colonial and post-colonial power. I'm indebted to his friendship, visits to his studio and conversations we have had along the way.

'The Ghazal of the Displaced' was fine-tuned in a Ghazal Workshop with Mona Arshi as part of Jerwood Compton Poetry Fellowship series, much love and thanks to Dr Nathalie Teitler.

'Lampedusa': "The captain of a rescue ship carrying 40 people has been arrested for breaking an Italian naval blockade that was trying to stop her from docking the vessel in Lampedusa. After a two-week standoff with Italian authorities, Carola Rackete, docked the German boat Sea-Watch 3." https://www.theguardian.com/world/2019/jun/29/sea-watch-captain-carola-rackete-arrested-italian-blockade

'Rio Grande': London, Wednesday 26 June 2019 *Evening Standard* Front Page Headline: "The Picture That Shames America; image of dead father and daughter shows horror of migrant crisis. How many times will we see images like this and still continue to put up borders?"

'Pantoum of the 27': for the 27 souls who lost their lives in the English Channel.

'Younous Chekkouri' was a commissioned poem in 2019 for Ledbury Poetry Festival and Reprieve, aimed to draw attention to the detainees still held in Guantanamo Bay. Reprieve founder and respected human rights lawyer, Clive Stafford Smith OBE hosted the event.

You are Impossible to Love (Part 2)
The vilification of Others and the removing people of colour or of a different culture from these shores has been a stain on the sensibilities of being British as can be seen in the following quotes: *"Those kinde of people should be sente forth of the land"* – Queen Elizabeth I (Letters Permitting Deportation of Blackamoors from England (1596)). *"…River Tiber foaming with much blood"* from the 'Rivers of Blood' speech by Enoch Powell (20th April 1968, to a meeting at the Conservative Political Centre in Birmingham). *"…this country might be rather swamped by people with a*

different culture" – Margaret Thatcher (from a TV Interview for Granada *World in Action*, 30th January, 1978).

I'm holding a scream is built around the prayer of Dutty Boukman and Cécile Fatiman, a Vodou priestess, who led a religious ceremony at Bois Caiman in August 1791, This, legend has it, was the spark that lit the Haitian revolution. Boukman and Fatiman prayed and inspired three hundred slaves to pledge to end slavery.

The god who created the earth; who created the sun that gives us light. The god who holds up the ocean; who makes the thunder roar. Our god who has ears to hear. You who are hidden in the clouds; who watch us from where you are. You see all that the white has made us suffer. The white man's god asks him to commit crimes. But the god within us wants to do good. Our god, who is so good, so just, He orders us to revenge our wrongs. It's He who will direct our arms and bring us the victory. It's He who will assist us. We all should throw away the image of the white men's god who is so pitiless. Listen to the voice for liberty that speaks in all our hearts.

Sources: https://en.wikipedia.org/wiki/Dutty_Boukman and also read https://vocalafrica.com/epic-dutty-boukman-story-prayer/.

The following Erasure & Inclusion (to make known) poems use text transcribed from the following original documents from the British Newspaper Archives (BNA) at the British Library:

'The Passion of the Enslaved / On the Body of a Negro': *Royal Gazette,* (Kingston, Jamaica) March 2nd, 1822

'Cain rose against Abel': *Barbados Mercury and Bridge-town Gazette* Tuesday 13th Jan 1818.

'Abel's blood cries from the ground': *Barbados Mercury and Bridge-town Gazette,* Saturday 21st February 1818.

'Abel, Hebel breath be thy name': *Barbados Mercury and Bridge-Town Gazette,* Saturday 9th May 1818.

'Threatened with Damnation': *Hampshire Independent,* Saturday 2nd September, 1848.

'Toussaint': *Hampshire Chronicle,* Monday 12th October 1801

'To be free': *Barbados Mercury and Bridge-Town Gazette,* Saturday 30th July 1814.

'Possession of the Kingdom': Account of the final abolition of slavery in England' from *The Scots Magazine,* Thursday 1st September 1808.

Acknowledgements and Thanks

Gratitude to the following for the temporary home given to many of my poems that appeared sometimes in different forms; *The Dark Horse, The Rialto, Poetry Birmingham Literary Journal, Magma* and *Ink, Sweat & Tears*.

Also 'Nanny of the Black Country wearing Converse All Stars' was winner of the Red Shed 2021 Poetry Competition. 'An Aubade in response to how do you feel…' was third place in the *Magma* Poetry Competition, 2020.

Many thanks for the following commissioned poems; 'After Hew Locke Wreck' for *A fine day for seeing; Ten Artists / Ten Poets* at Southwark Galleries. '…Ira Aldridge is often visited by his Spirit' for BBC Contains Strong Language as part of Coventry City of Culture 2021.

Special thanks to the Eccles Centre for American Studies at the British Library and Dr Cara Rodway; to The Society of Authors and Authors Foundation for the Emergency Fund during Covid, and the Arthur Welton Award.

I'm indebted to everyone who helped me along the way with this third collection during unprecedented times. Paul Grant, Phil Simpson & Trevor Dawkins for always challenging, and drawing out the nostalgia and the countless memories. A special holler to Denzil Fletcher recovering from a major illness. Hew Locke & Indra Khanna for their friendship and book cover. Tamar Yoseloff, Mary Mulholland, Liz Berry, Jonathan Davidson & Zellig Poets. Nick Makoha and the fellowship and love from the Obsidian Foundation. Fiona Bennett & John Prebble for watching over me during dark times. Huge gratitude to Dante Micheaux a main source of motivation and support in the making of this book.

Finally, many thanks to Jane Commane my publisher, and to Maish my loving partner for understanding the early morning risings with the muse and those homemade banana cakes and tea that kept me going.

Further Reading:

Alabanza: New and Selected Poems 1982-2002, Martín Espada (W. W. Norton, & Co., 2004).

A Humument: A Treated Victorian Novel, Tom Phillips (Thames and Hudson Ltd, 1980).

All The Names Given, Raymond Antrobus (Picador, 2021).

Brilliant Corners, Nuzhat Bukhari (CB Editions, 2021).

Folk Culture Of The Slaves In Jamaica, Edward Kamau Braithwaite (New Beacon Books, 1981).

Just Us: An American Conversation, Claudia Rankine (Penguin, 2021).

Jamaica, Andrew Salkey (Hutchinson, 1973).

neck|bone, avery r. young (Northwestern University Press, 2019).

New Slaveries In Contemporary British Literature And Visual Arts, Pietro Deandrea (Manchester University Press, 2015).

Researching Race and Racism, eds. Martin Bulmer & John Solomos (Routledge, 2004).

Staying Power: The History of Black People in Britain, Peter Fryer (Pluto Press, 2018).